this book belongs to

joy

comes
in the
morning

60 DEVOTIONS TO START YOUR DAY

Ellie
Claire®

gift & paper expressions

Ellie Claire® Gift & Paper Expressions
Franklin, TN 37067
EllieClaire.com
Ellie Claire is a registered trademark of Worthy Media, Inc.

Joy Comes in the Morning: 60 Devotions to Start Your Day
© 2016 by Ellie Claire
Published by Ellie Claire, an imprint of Worthy Publishing Group, a division of
Worthy Media, Inc.

ISBN 978-1-63326-151-8

Typesetting by Jeff Jansen | aestheticsoup.net

Printed in China

1 2 3 4 5 6 7 8 9 HAHA 21 20 19 18 17 16

The whole earth is filled
with awe at your wonders;
where morning dawns,
where evening fades,
you call forth songs of joy.

The Faith to Celebrate

Elijah said to Ahab, "Go up, eat and drink,
for there is the sound of a rainstorm."

1 KINGS 18:41 HCSB

*T*hough things don't always go as planned, we find security in knowing that there are some things we can count on—like the sunrise, for instance. Very few of us go to sleep wondering whether the sun will come up in the morning. It always does. We count on it.

Even more than the rising of the sun, you can count on God's faithfulness every day and in any circumstance. That doesn't mean that everything will happen according to your wishes, but it does mean that God can and will work with everything that happens.

The next time you find yourself in a situation where things aren't going your way, accept the situation as an opportunity to engage with God in exercise of true faith. Go to Him in prayer and ask Him for insight and understanding regarding your circumstances, realizing that His will can be accomplished through adversity as well as ease.

As you gain more insight and understanding, you'll move deeper into faith and begin to celebrate the outcome in advance. Those who know God know that He will champion His people. It's just a matter of time. So even if things aren't exactly as you wish, trust the Lord knowing that He will always be there, day in and day out to make the best of what the day brings.

Trusting that You are faithful, Lord,
I need to begin celebrating right now over...

Have courage
for the great sorrows
of life and patience
for the small ones;
and when you have
laboriously accomplished
your daily task,
go to sleep in peace.
God is awake.

VICTOR HUGO

Rhythm of Relationship

Seven times a day I praise you.
PSALM 119:164 NIV

God loves to be with you, but He doesn't demand 100 percent of your time. He gives you room to think, to explore, to create, to relax, to be yourself. There is a rhythm in a relationship with God. Yes, He is always here to sustain you, to protect you, to provide for you. But He doesn't expect intense worship and attention from you 24/7. He knows you need time to work, read books, pay bills, buy groceries, have coffee with a friend, tuck the children into bed, or whatever. Even in Eden, unspoiled perfection, God gave us our space. He walked with Adam and Eve in the cool part of the day.

Many of us have chosen a certain part of the day for spending time alone with God. For some it works well to make it first thing in the morning. Others prefer a different time. Some people take shorter times to meet with God several times throughout the day. You may find that one system works well in one season of your life but needs to be adjusted in another. We are always available to God, and He is always available to us. But our focused time together follows a pattern or a rhythm. That is exactly what He intended.

When You meet with me, God, I'm grateful that…

I am convinced
beyond a shadow
of any doubt
that the most
valuable pursuit
we can embark upon
is to know God.

KAY ARTHUR

Winning Warrior

You give us victory over our enemies,
you put our adversaries to shame.

PSALM 44:7 NIV

*T*here is a winner's DNA inside you. Even when you've endured awful things, there is a spark within you that resists giving in to defeat. It's the thing that makes you get up again after being knocked down. It's the inner warrior that refuses to quit and puts on the gear for one more go-round.

God salutes that. He is cheering you on, inspiring you to stand up. Defeating something big in your life that's been hounding you is God's line of work. Take a minute and think about your picture of God. In that view, has He ever lost? Are the forces against Him ever bigger or greater than He is? Have you heard any stories about that time God almost made it but went down in the last round? No! Those stories don't exist. God is the most decorated warrior in history.

So, does God care about your battles? Emphatically, yes. God cares and is on your side for your success. Your God is a God who saves. He is a tide-turner and a game-changer. When you're up against it, ask Him how to respond like the winner He's making you to be. Then be alert for His encouragement.

Lord, I have noticed little encouragements from You in…

Be of good cheer. Do not think
of today's failures, but of
the success that may come tomorrow.
You have set yourselves a difficult task,
but you will succeed if you persevere;
and you will find a joy in
overcoming obstacles. Remember,
no effort that we make to attain
something beautiful is ever lost.

HELEN KELLER

Embrace Simplicity

Satisfy us in the morning with your unfailing love,
that we may sing for joy and be glad all our days.

PSALM 90:14 NIV

"Embracing simplicity" doesn't mean living on a subsistence level. It does mean seeing the material trappings of life as mere adornment—and finding true peace and fulfillment in your relationship with God and in those qualities that He has placed within you.

Most of us realize that mere survival is not what God intended for His people. However, the abundance we enjoy on the outside can blind us to the spiritual abundance God has provided for us. What does that mean? It means that God offers each of us the gifts and grace we need to make the most of the life we've been given and help others do the same without having to rely on material possessions for contentment.

The place to begin is in your personal time alone with God. It is there in His presence that you will see the bigger picture. When viewed from the perspective of eternity, many of the concerns of this material world will diminish in importance. Ask God to give you the grace to live in anticipation of the joys that are to come. When you do, you will find life to be so much simpler.

Dear God, today I will embrace simplicity by…

Happy people...enjoy the fundamental,
often very simple things of life....
They savor the moment, glad to be alive,
enjoying their work, their families,
the good things around them.
They are adaptable; they can bend
with the wind, adjust to the changes
in their times, enjoy the contest of life....
Their eyes are turned outward;
they are aware, compassionate.
They have the capacity to love.

JANE CANFIELD

Thirst for God

Let them give thanks to the LORD...for he satisfies
the thirsty and fills the hungry with good things.
PSALM 107:8–9 NIV

Do you ever feel restless? Unsatisfied?

Unfulfilled longings are a common human experience. But at the heart of every longing is a thirst for God. No matter what you desire, your desires can only be ultimately satisfied in Him. In fact, He promises to satisfy your desires with good things. A life partner, a new car, a different job, a better marriage—all these things can be good, but only God gives the kind of foundational contentment that makes all of life bearable.

The Bible describes followers of God who suffered imprisonment and all sorts of persecution as being filled with an indescribable joy. How is that possible? It isn't, apart from God. When your thirst for God is satisfied, nothing else matters.

Reach out to God in prayer. As He fills up all the empty places in your heart, His love will overflow to others, even to the unlovable; His joy will bubble up, even in the midst of grief; His peace will guard you, even when you are surrounded by turmoil.

God, I thirst for...

The thought of You
stirs us so deeply
that we cannot be content
unless we praise You,
because You have made us
for Yourself and our hearts
find no peace until
they rest in You.

AUGUSTINE

God's Biggest Fan

O God, You are my God; early will I seek You;
my soul thirsts for You; my flesh longs for You
in a dry and thirsty land where there is no water.

PSALM 63:1 NKJV

The sports fan is an interesting animal. He or she may not recall vital information such as his ATM number or the location of his car keys, but his brain will instantly conjure up Magic Johnson's alma mater, the co-MVPs of Super Bowl XII, or the team the Dodgers beat the last time they won the World Series. Why does this phenomenon occur? Because people tend to easily remember those things that bring them joy and relaxation.

Knowing God and communicating with Him in prayer should be, at minimum, as pleasurable to you as, say, an evening of watching game highlights is to the sports fan. Actually, recalling what God reveals to you in your prayer time and applying it to who you are is to be your delight!

Don't let your relationship with God and praying to Him be mere duty. Allow God's wisdom to be your life's fun and joy—and join His fan club!

God, I enjoy being with You because…

There is no joy
comparable to the joy
of discovering something
new from God, about God.
If the continuing life
is a life of joy,
we will go on discovering,
learning.

EUGENIA PRICE

Live your life
while you have it.
Life is a splendid gift —
there is nothing small
about it.

Florence Nightingale

You, a Conqueror

Everyone born of God overcomes the world.
This is the victory that has overcome the world, even our faith.

1 JOHN 5:4 NIV

What's your image of a conqueror? History buffs may think of someone like Alexander the Great, who conquered much of the known world of his time, or Attila the Hun, who subdued most of Europe in the fifth century A.D. But you too can be a conqueror—not by ruthlessly taking over a geographical area, but by relentlessly warring against the spiritual forces that try to bring you down.

Those forces take many forms: the devastating effects of a drug culture that continually tries to entice your children to join in its addictions, the hidden habits of your own heart that tempt you to deny your marriage vows, the unforgiveness that prevents you from living a joyful life in God's presence. The good news, however, is that God has given you everything you need to overcome whatever the world throws your way. That "everything" is Jesus Christ and your faith in Him.

The faith that conquers the world—those spiritual forces that oppose you—is simply an abiding trust that God will do what He has said He will do. Take God at His word. His power working in and through you is all you need to become the conqueror He said you can be.

Mighty God, help me become a conqueror in…

Hope floods my heart
with delight! Running on air,
mad with life, dizzy, reeling,
upward I mount—faith is sight,
life is feeling.... I am immortal!
I know it! I feel it!

MARGARET WITTER FULLER

Life's Lessons

The LORD is a refuge for the oppressed,
a refuge in times of trouble.

PSALM 9:9 HCSB

Where do we learn life's real lessons? Usually it is not when the crowds are cheering, money is in the bank, and we feel great. Rather, we learn lessons when a friend disappoints us, the job ends, the report from the doctor isn't good. It's in these difficult times that we find that we need to turn to Someone greater than ourselves.

Are you in the middle of one of those challenging times right now? First of all, know this: Even when others don't understand, God does. He is here, ready right now to listen to everything that is in your heart. God is the best listener in the universe. But He is more than that. He will share life-changing truth with us if we are willing to listen. That truth can come in many forms: a phone call from a friend, a new discovery from the Bible, a circumstance with God's unmistakable fingerprints on it, a quiet internal conviction that He is speaking.

None of us enjoy going through hard times, but most of us can point back to these trials as the time when we grew the most as people. Take the journey with God, and know that you will emerge triumphant.

Dear Lord, in challenging times, it helps me to remember…

God has not promised
sun without rain, joy without sorrow,
peace without pain. But God has
promised strength for the day,
rest for the labor, light for the way,
grace for the trials, help from above,
unfailing sympathy, undying love.

ANNIE JOHNSON FLINT

Never Forget

In the future, when your children ask their fathers,
"What is the meaning of these stones?" you should tell
your children, "Israel crossed the Jordan on dry ground."

JOSHUA 4:21–22 HCSB

When God delivers, never forget what He's done for you. When He rescues you from danger, remember that day. When He delivers you from a bad work situation, remember that day. When He provides the help you needed, remember that day. And then, share the story.

We tend to have short memories. Even major events are forgotten, as many a wife will attest regarding her husband's memory of anniversaries. Remembering what God has done for you builds your faith. Sharing the story builds faith for others.

Create your own memorials. One of the simplest ways is to keep a journal. Write a log of your journey, the joy and the trouble, and then how God showed up in the middle of it. If it's been a long-awaited moment, celebrate it with friends over a special meal and highlight God's awesome rescue. Or you could make a cairn in your garden, setting stones on top of each other as a memorial. The point is not what you choose to do, but to do something to help you remember in days to come. God is a good God who rescues His people. Remember, and tell the story.

Lord, I want to remember what You did when…

Gratitude unlocks the fullness of life.
It turns what we have into enough,
and more.... It can turn a meal into
a feast, a house into a home,
a stranger into a friend.
Gratitude makes sense of our past,
brings peace for today,
and creates a vision for tomorrow.

MELODY BEATTIE

Undercover Boss

*When all our enemies heard about this…[they] were afraid
and lost their self-confidence, because they realized
that this work had been done with the help of our God.*

NEHEMIAH 6:16 NIV

God is a great manager. He is ready to help His people. The almighty God desires your success. When asked, He gets in the middle of the muddled times, carrying you through the muck until you are on solid ground again. He infuses your work with life. People see it. Those who love life are drawn to your cause. They know there's more to you and your work than meets the eye, and they can see God reflected in your passion and purpose.

God enjoys empowering you. He loves seeing a good plan succeed. Invite Him into your latest project. Work in a way that honors Him. It's so easy to cut a corner or leave out a detail, but God doesn't—and He loves excellence in His people. Humbly recognize God's authority over everything and His amazing management ability. Imagine that He's right by your side as you labor. Dedicate your best to each minute of your work. Your attitude and trust invites God to move in and do something greater than you could do on your own.

God, recognizing Your authority, I will…

Each one of us is God's
special work of art.
Through us, He teaches
and inspires, delights
and encourages, informs
and uplifts all those
who view our lives.

JONI EARECKSON TADA

Restoring the Joy

Why, my soul, are you downcast? Why so disturbed within me?
Put your hope in God, for I will yet praise him,
my Savior and my God.

PSALM 42:5 NIV

How's your energy? Are you feeling in tune with God and with yourself, or is this a day when things feel a little off? Some days you must give yourself a good talking to just to get out the door. Your head starts filling with cynical thinking and out goes your joy. It's a challenge to find peace.

Those negative ideas are straight from the pit. They don't help or energize you, but they sure do paint your day gray. They're often believable enough to sound like truth, but if you only focus on that negativity, it will weigh you down, steal your dreams, and discourage your heart. And the more you believe it, the worse your day will seem.

Instead of listening to the lies, grab those thoughts and replace them with uplifting statements that are true and good! Refuse to dwell on thoughts of failure. You are an overcomer, connected to the almighty God. He is able to turn around your situation in a heartbeat, and all it costs you is faith.

Hang on to your hope. Re-center, and remember you are God's child. Remember that He is a life-giver. And when you do, you'll have plenty to be glad about again.

God, help me to focus on positive and uplifting thoughts about…

God shall be my hope,
my stay,
my guide and lantern
to my feet.

WILLIAM SHAKESPEARE

A Voyage of Wonder

*I beseech you therefore, brethren, by the mercies of God,
that you present your bodies a living sacrifice, holy,
acceptable to God, which is your reasonable service.*

ROMANS 12:1 NKJV

In a sense, all of life is a prayer, a voyage of discovery, if you allow it to be. If you throw open the doors to let God in, you will find that you want to live every moment, waking or sleeping, as a love offering to Him. This need not be overly mystical. Rather, it's as practical as saying, "Here I am. My life belongs to You. I give this day to you."

The Bible encourages this kind of prayer when it instructs us to present ourselves as a living sacrifice to God. For some people, this is challenging because they focus on what they give up: their right to be the final authority in their lives. But for others, this is pure joy, their life's highest calling: an opportunity to delight the heart of God Himself.

If you have trouble handing God the keys to your life, ask God to reveal who He is to you. With each new glimpse of His beauty, you'll want to give Him more of yourself. And life will become a voyage of wonder and discovery.

God, I believe deep inside that You really are…

Prayer is such an ordinary,
everyday, mundane thing. Certainly,
people who pray are no more saints
than the rest of us. Rather,
they are people who want to share
a life with God, to love and be loved,
to speak and to listen, to work
and to be at rest in the presence of God.

ROBERTA BONDI

The greater part of our happiness or misery depends upon our dispositions, and not upon our circumstances.

MARTHA WASHINGTON

The Gift of Mercy

*He arose and came to his father. But when he was
still a great way off, his father saw him and had compassion,
and ran and fell on his neck and kissed him.*

LUKE 15:20 NKJV

"Mercy" is a word that isn't used much in ordinary conversation today. Maybe that's because there's something about it that sounds old-fashioned, conjuring up an image of a nineteenth-century woman crying "Mercy!" at the sight of an exposed ankle. But maybe the word isn't used much today because mercy—withholding punishment from someone who deserves it—is in such short supply. Wherever a wrong has been committed, you'll find people who want the perpetrator punished *beyond* the full extent of the law.

The problem with unmerciful thinking is that when we practice it, we probably don't realize how often we've been on the receiving end of mercy. As children, we likely received mercy from our parents, our teachers, or other people in authority when we did something deserving punishment. As adults, we may have received mercy from a boss without even realizing it.

Every person, no matter their age, has received mercy from God. Mercy is a gift He lavishes on His people despite our disobedience, our rebellion, and our disregard of His many blessings. You can be one of those who acknowledge that gift by expressing your gratitude to God for the many times—seen and unseen—that He has shown mercy to you.

God, I acknowledge that You have shown mercy to me by…

For God is, indeed,
a wonderful Father
who longs to pour out
His mercy upon us,
and whose majesty
is so great that He can
transform us from
deep within.

Teresa of Avila

Feelings Could Talk

Bring joy to your servant, Lord, for I put my trust in you.
PSALM 86:4 NIV

If your feelings could talk, what would they say?

Like children who blurt out whatever is on their minds, feelings convey the very contents of our souls. *I am deeply loved. I'm ugly. No one cares. Life is beautiful. Things are going my way. I'm trapped and all alone. Life is unfair.*

Those messages and those beliefs may or may not be true; they may or may not reflect reality. But they are there, and deep inside we have reasons for coming to those conclusions. All of this provides an opportunity for God to reveal His truth. As you come into His presence and let your feelings talk, hold these buried messages up to Him, and, if you can, you tell Him how you came to your conclusions. Then you look up into the face of God and ask, "Is it true? Am I really ugly? Will I never amount to anything? What is the truth?"

That is when the transformation comes. That is when you learn the soul-cleansing truth. It is the truth for you and for all of us. We really are beautiful, deeply loved, fully capable sons and daughters of God.

If my feelings could talk, they would say…

Though our feelings
come and go,
God's love for us
does not.

C. S. LEWIS

Greater than His Gifts

*Think about Him in all your ways,
and He will guide you on the right paths.*
PROVERBS 3:6 HCSB

As you think through God's many gifts, do you ever stop to ask which is the greatest of all? Would it be the health God provides? Or would His greatest gift be family, friends, and relationships? Then again, the peace and joy, opportunities and strength God grants are all priceless. But there is a gift that rises to the top and towers over everything else that God can give. That gift is God Himself. The greatest answer to prayer is not healing or a miracle or a million dollars. The greatest answer to prayer is God Himself because God is greater than His gifts.

By seeking God first in your prayers, you invite Him to journey through life with you, even if you never get healed or get out of debt or get that perfect marriage or family that you desire. For the man or woman who is patient in prayer, God shows up and all His other gifts eventually follow. The presence of the Giver gives every other gift its value.

God, I value You over Your gifts because…

Open wide the windows
of our spirits and fill us
full of light; open wide
the door of our hearts
that we may receive
and entertain Thee
with all the powers
of our adoration.

CHRISTINA ROSSETTI

The God Who Sings

[God] will rejoice over you with singing.
ZEPHANIAH 3:17 NKJV

When holding a newborn in their arms, proud parents and grandparents coo like a baby, talk like a baby, and regardless of their degree of musical ability, they sing. Proud parents and grandparents have few inhibitions.

Did you know that God feels the same way about you—even in your old age? The Bible says He delights in you. That means when He thinks of you, He is overcome with joy. He is so overwhelmed with love for you that He sings over you, just like a loving father unabashedly sings over his child. God's truest desires are unrestrained where His children are concerned.

Think about the song He is singing over you. Listen for it when you are in quiet prayer, waiting in His presence. It's a song that brings you peace in the midst of distress. It's a song filled with warm affection. It's a song describing the joy He feels when He calls you His own. Listen to it. Believe in it. It is your song; a song He wrote for you alone.

Lord God, when I hear a whisper of Your song over me, I will…

If God had a refrigerator,
your picture would be on it.
If He had a wallet,
your photo would be in it.
He sends you flowers
every spring and a sunrise
every morning... Face it, friend.
He is crazy about you!

MAX LUCADO

God's Great Heart

The LORD bless you and keep you; the LORD make
his face shine on you and be gracious to you;
the LORD turn his face toward you and give you peace.

NUMBERS 6:24–26 NIV

Are you aware of God's desire to fill your life with an abundance of good things?

God wants to bless you. It is His greatest joy to give lavishly and generously to those whom He loves—and His love is indiscriminate. Are you receptive to God's blessing, aware that in relationship with God you are also in a position to experience His abundance?

God cares for you. Even concerning the smallest details of your day, it matters to the Lord that things are well with you. Did you know that He is with you to bless you when things go wrong, as well as when things go right? God gives you peace. Though this world is a troubled place, the Lord provides the calm that allows you to pillow your head at night, confident that you'll arise in the morning. Do you trust Him when your peace is disturbed?

God is attentive to you. He doesn't miss anything. Are you reciprocally attentive to Him? God prospers you. He rewards and applauds your efforts. Do you return thanks? God smiles on you. Observant and always looking for the best in you, God looks for reasons to rejoice over you. Did you know that you bless His heart with joy?

I want to thank You, God, for all You give me by…

A life contemplating
the blessings of Christ
becomes a life acting
the love of Christ.

ANN VOSKAMP

A Turn in Perspective

*Our light and momentary troubles are achieving for us
an eternal glory that far outweighs them all.*
2 CORINTHIANS 4:17 NIV

A scene in the classic movie *Steel Magnolias* shows four women gathered around their dear friend at the gravesite of her daughter. The mother is distraught and cannot quit shouting, "Why? Why did my daughter have to die?" Then one of the older women cracks a joke. Her friends look at her stunned, but after a short pause, they all burst out laughing.

What changed their outlook? Their thoughts were given a different focus! In the Bible, we read that King David often felt utterly forsaken, sorrowful, and under attack. He'd even question God, "How long will it be this way?" Yet David's thoughts always turned toward the benefits of God in his life, especially the undeserved and unfailing mercy God gave to him.

When you have trying times, change your thinking. No matter how bleak circumstances appear, pray that you may have God's perspective, seeing life as He does. Reflect the joy in your heart for God's bountiful blessings. Praise Him. Then pray with thanksgiving.

I thank You, God, and pray for new perspective concerning…

God is every moment
totally aware of each one of us.
Totally aware in intense
concentration and love....
No one passes through
any area of life,
happy or tragic,
without the attention of God.

EUGENIA PRICE

Weeping
may endure
for a night,
but joy comes
in the morning.

PSALM 30:5 NKJV

Your Prayer of Triumph

May we shout for joy when we hear of your victory
and raise a victory banner in the name of our God.
May the LORD answer all your prayers.

*S*ooner or later, you win because you are on the winning team—
you are a son or daughter of God. Triumph is your destiny. Success
is your birthright as a member of God's royal family. That will look
a little different for each person, but in the things that really matter,
you win.

The great men and women of the Bible remembered that their
success came from somewhere outside themselves. In their moment
of triumph, they paused to acknowledge God's greatness. When He
gives you the victory you desire or grants you the ability you need,
remember all of your provision comes from His hand.

If you are in the daily habit of praising God for His goodness in
your life, your success will be yet another opportunity to see life
from His perspective.

God, because of You, I am triumphant in…

Let us give all
that lies within us...
to pure praise,
to pure loving adoration,
and to worship from
a grateful heart—
a heart that is trained
to look up.

AMY CARMICHAEL

In the Midst of Sickness

*May the God of hope fill you with all joy
and peace as you trust in him.*

ROMANS 15:13 NIV

From our perspective, ongoing sickness doesn't make a great deal of sense. How on earth can pain and suffering be good? Equally frustrating can be our continuous pleas to God for relief while He seems to do nothing.

Some of the godliest people in the Bible suffered prolonged sickness or disease. Job lost his children to tragic deaths, his belongings were destroyed, and he was stricken with painful sores all over his body. Yet the Bible tells us that God considered him "blameless and upright." A young pastor named Timothy suffered from frequent stomach problems, yet to our knowledge he never experienced relief from the pain.

This tells us that we cannot make a direct correlation between godliness and sickness.

We must make peace with the fact that godly people suffer.

Never draw back from asking God to heal you. But as you bring your request, ask also that your eyes be opened to His goodness, and then trust that He is indeed doing something good in you.

God, open my eyes to see Your goodness in the midst of…

My trust in God flows out
of the experience of His loving me,
day in and day out, whether the day is
stormy or fair, whether I'm sick
or in good health, whether I'm in a state
of grace or disgrace. He comes to me
where I live and loves me as I am.

BRENNAN MANNING

Experiencing Pure Joy

You will live in joy and peace. The mountains and hills will burst into song, and the trees of the field will clap their hands!

ISAIAH 55:12 NLT

Do you know that you can experience true joy even when things aren't going your way? Some people don't understand the difference between happiness and joy, so when circumstances rob them of their happiness, they think joy automatically disappears too. But you can still have a deep, abiding joy even when happiness eludes you, because, while happiness is tied to your circumstances, joy is closely linked to your relationship with God.

Joy sees the world through the eyes of faith. Here's one example of what that means: Your physical eyes may look in the mirror and see someone who's aging much too quickly, and that doesn't make you very happy. But your eyes of faith see a person whom God has blessed with many years, and you joyfully determine that you are going to make the best of the years that are left no matter what happens, blessing Him in return.

Your eyes of faith help you to see that the things that so often bring people down are of little consequence in comparison to the joy that comes from knowing God—and knowing that there's nothing on earth that can rob you of that joy.

I can experience pure joy right now because…

If it can be verified,
we don't need faith....
Faith is for that which lies
on the other side of reason.
Faith is what makes
life bearable,
with all its tragedies
and ambiguities
and sudden, startling joys.

MADELEINE L'ENGLE

The Times of Your Life

Though I walk in the midst of trouble, you preserve my life.
PSALM 138:7 NIV

Keeping a log of God's timely answers to your prayers is an uplifting practice. But what about the times when you don't see your prayers answered? What do you do when you find yourself feeling sad and disappointed? Should you record those times as well? Of course you should.

The Lord allows and even desires for you to declare such honest emotion. But He also loves when you trust Him. Even the prophet Jeremiah, often called the weeping prophet because of the despair he faced, cried out, "Great is Your faithfulness!" In his times of overwhelming sadness, he still knew the Lord was in control and would see him through to the end.

God will see you through as well. He has promised to stay by your side through joy and sorrow. He has promised never to leave you no matter what. Bring everything to Him and experience His joy, comfort, and faithfulness.

The difficulties I'm giving to You today, Lord, are…

The more you go
with the flow of life
and surrender the outcome to God,
and the less you seek
constant clarity, the more
you will find that
fabulous things start
to show up in your life.

MANDY HALE

When Life Is Good

Seek the LORD and His strength; seek His face evermore!
1 CHRONICLES 16:11 NKJV

*M*any people cry out to God in desperate times. When times are good? Not so much.

While reaching for God in our hardship is always beneficial, maintaining the same mindset during prosperous times is equally important. The approach, however, may be different.

In times of difficulty, we tend to ask God to intervene in our lives, so our prayers take the form of a request. When we experience those all-too-rare moments when problems seem like a distant memory, our prayers can take the form of thanksgiving. Granted, requests and thanksgiving aren't mutually exclusive, but prayer is often dominated by one or the other.

Keeping the communication lines open with God when life is good is a reminder that you need Him. Always. God is your provider, encourager, and the giver of life. Without Him you would have nothing and be nothing. And thanking Him in seasons of abundance helps you remember that. Ultimately, it reminds you that you're not alone. Everything good in your life comes directly from your loving heavenly Father.

Lord God, thank You for blessing me with…

If it is God who gives prayer,
then God often gives it
in the form of gratitude,
and gratitude itself,
when it is received
attentively in prayer,
is healing to the heart.
Prayer is such a mysterious
business for something
so ordinary and everyday.

ROBERTA BONDI

Finding the Ability to Bless

David returned home to bless his household.
2 Samuel 6:20 niv

Where do we find the capacity to bless those closest to us? How do we find the ability to speak life-giving words of hope and encouragement to those around us? What needs to happen in us so that our actions nurture those in our circle of influence?

In a sense, the answer is simple: You can't pour water from an empty pitcher. We need to find "the blessing" ourselves. We need to be filled up to overflowing inside before we can pour affirming love out on others.

Some of us are fortunate enough to have real or surrogate parents who communicated to us, "I love you just as you are. I believe in you. You matter." Some of us are not that fortunate. But, ultimately, for all of us, our "blessing" and affirmation come from God Himself. This is why it is so important that you let yourself be loved by God.

Linger in His presence and let Him share with you the joy He feels that you are you. Drink in the love of God. From that place, you will be empowered to go into your world and touch people with the life-changing presence and love of Christ.

I experience Your love, God, when…

If you took the love of all the best
mothers and fathers who ever lived
(think about that for a moment) –
all the goodness, kindness, patience,
fidelity, wisdom, tenderness, strength
and love – and united all those virtues
in one person, that person would only be
a faint shadow of the love and mercy
in the heart of God for you and me.

BRENNAN MANNING

Where the soul
is full of peace and joy,
outward surroundings
and circumstances
are of comparatively
little account.

HANNAH WHITALL SMITH

God's Abundance

Why do you spend money on what is not food,
and your wages on what does not satisfy? Listen carefully to Me,
and eat what is good, and you will enjoy the choicest of foods.

Isaiah 55:2 HCSB

If you're like most people in the world, you're not living in the lap of luxury. And abundance? What's that? All you ever seem to see an abundance of is bills.

The reality is that you can experience abundance—and may already be experiencing it—though it may not be the kind of abundance that comes to mind immediately. Look at the people in your life; are you rich in friends, relatives, people who care about you? Look at your possessions; do you have anything beyond what is necessary to sustain life? Look at your environment; do you see evidence of God's goodness anywhere in your immediate surroundings? Look at what is stored inside of you; are you rich in the treasures you've discovered as you've spent time with God and His Word?

You may never have an abundance of wealth in this lifetime. That's all right. Accumulating wealth is not a godly goal in and of itself anyway. But you can still enjoy God's abundance—in the people He has placed in your life, in His promise of provision, in the world He created for you to enjoy, and in the wisdom He has given you as a guide for your life.

Dear God, I will show You my gratitude for Your abundance by…

Whatsoever is good
for God's children
they shall have it;
for all is theirs
to help them
towards heaven.

RICHARD SIBBES

The Icebreaker

Give praise to the LORD, proclaim his name;
make known among the nations what he has done.
1 CHRONICLES 16:8 NIV

In polar regions, a special class of ships known as icebreakers move through ice-covered water, creating a path for other ships to follow. Without icebreakers, navigation in some areas would be impossible.

The discipline of giving thanks acts like an icebreaker in your soul, clearing a path for hope and joy to follow. Thanksgiving refocuses your attention on God's ultimate victory, on the good gifts He brings into your life, and on His ability to use even negative circumstances for your benefit. Thanksgiving affirms your understanding that you are on the winning team, that loss and pain are not your final destiny, that God knows how to wipe away every tear.

As you thank God, even in the midst of distressing situations, His comforting presence draws near, and clarity about the things that really matter begins to emerge. You understand that in God you are indestructible and at His side you will prevail. You see that literally nothing can separate you from God's love, and in that love you will be and are okay.

God, I thank You for…

No matter what
our circumstance,
we can find a reason
to be thankful.

DAVID JEREMIAH

Singing the Blues

Those who have been ransomed by the LORD will return.
They will enter Jerusalem singing, crowned with
everlasting joy. Sorrow and mourning will disappear,
and they will be filled with joy and gladness.

ISAIAH 35:10 NLT

How do you work through your anxiety, grief, or discouragement? Rather than succumb to unhealthy habits and behaviors, it's best to have a strategy that will serve you well when unpleasant emotions come calling.

The Bible tells us that the people of ancient Israel understood the importance of acknowledging their negative emotions. Often, the people recited prayers and sang songs called laments. A lament is a song or poem that expresses anxiety, grief, discouragement, or any other negative emotion. The Bible is full of them. One book—Lamentations—is a lament in five stanzas.

Laments are actually similar to what we call singing the blues. When you're dealing with negative emotions, put what you're feeling into words and get them out in the open. Then when you're through singing the blues, begin to sing praise to God, for He is the one who can turn your sadness and frustration into joy and hope for the future.

Heavenly Father, the lament I want to sing today is about…

Heartache forces us
to embrace God
out of desperate, urgent need.
God is never closer than
when your heart is aching.

JONI EARECKSON TADA

Fresh Strength

Those who hope in the LORD will renew their strength.
They will soar on wings like eagles; they will run
and not grow weary, they will walk and not be faint.

ISAIAH 40:31 NIV

On the soccer field, the lop-sided loss tastes bitter to the six-year-old. He didn't mean to score one for the other team. Dejected by the final outcome and by his own performance, the boy trudges off the field. But suddenly, he spots his dad waiting at the edge of the field. The father gently reaches for his son's hand. Hope quietly resurges in the youngster as he clenches his father's sure grip.

Your heavenly Father is reaching for your hand too. He knows you work hard. He knows you give your all but sometimes come up short. He knows when you're worn out by life and feel faint in your faith. God understands when you feel like crawling into a hole or plopping down in defeat. When you feel like you've endured one too many lop-sided losses, God wants you to simply put your hand in His—and trust. He promises to exchange His strength for your weariness.

So what are you holding on to these days? Are your fingers wrapped around your relationships, your work, your social calendar? What or whom are you trusting in for hope, renewal, and vitality? Put your trust in the One who longs to revive you with fresh strength.

Lord, I need fresh strength for…

When a man has
no strength,
if he leans on God,
he becomes powerful.

D. L. MOODY

Color Your Life

*You reveal the path of life to me; in Your presence
is abundant joy; in Your right hand are eternal pleasures.*

PSALM 16:11 HCSB

Many people spend each day merely surviving in their relationships and spiritual life. They go through the motions, waving good-bye as they leave for work, making dinner plans, going to kids' activities. But they've lost a deeper connection. There could be more, but it just seems too much of an effort to try.

If you or someone you know is in survival mode, it's time to take a bold step toward a greater quality of life. It might be uncomfortable at first, but true contentment is hard to find in mediocrity. Prayer is a great place to start. Praying alone, or with your spouse or children, will help you cut through the murky routine of simply getting through life and take you to the deeper, more significant, more fulfilling areas of your personal life and your relationships.

As you listen and learn about these areas and then give them to God, asking for His purposes to be accomplished, life will take on new color. It'll become vibrant, renewed, and anything but mediocre.

God, I will courageously move from survival to fulfillment by…

The Creator thinks enough
of you to have sent
Someone very special
so that you might
have life—abundantly,
joyfully, completely,
and victoriously.

The Glory to Come

I consider that our present sufferings are not worth comparing with the glory that will be revealed in us.
ROMANS 8:18 NIV

The fullness of God's glory, which we will one day see, is far greater than the most majestic scene you've ever witnessed on earth— brighter than the sun, even. The glory of God is one of the few things that can truly be described as awesome. It's so far beyond our human comprehension that our feeble attempts to envision it fall ridiculously short. We simply can't imagine it. We'll have to wait until we can experience it.

When we enter into the glory of God, we will also enter a dimension in which we will receive everything that God has for us— our eternal inheritance of healing, joy, peace, transformation, righteousness, and so much more. In the presence of God's glory, there will be no more suffering, pain, mourning, tears, or death. We'll be so transformed that even if we couldn't sing a note on earth, we'll sing praises to God right along with a choir of angels.

Each time you praise God in the midst of suffering or hardship of any kind, you're preparing for that day when every painful experience will disappear in the brilliant light of God's glory—and you'll receive your inheritance.

When I consider Your glory, God, I think of…

How sweet is rest
after fatigue!
How sweet will
heaven be when
our journey is ended.

GEORGE WHITEFIELD

Hope begins in the dark, the stubborn hope that if you just show up and try to do the right thing, the dawn will come. You wait and watch and work: You don't give up.

ANNE LAMOTT

Break Down the Wall

God…reconciled us to himself through Christ
and gave us the ministry of reconciliation.

2 CORINTHIANS 5:18 NIV

*H*ave you ever been so mad at someone that you didn't want to apologize for your actions or words? Did you ever need to ask your child for forgiveness for your angry outburst, but hesitated? There is a wall between the two of you, a barrier that, left unaddressed, could eventually destroy that relationship.

This is where God's incredible love for you makes an impact. He took the initiative to provide, at terrible cost, the ultimate avenue for restoration. He sent His Son. Belief that Jesus loves you, forgives you, and lives in you restores you to a harmonious relationship with God and enables you to then practice that same restoration in your life's most important relationships. Forgiveness is possible because you have been forgiven.

What could give you greater joy than to break down that wall? Strive to live Jesus's love in all that you do toward others. Apologize when you need to and seek restoration—starting with your prayers. Discover the pleasure of being at peace with others and with God.

Help me to apologize, God, to…

Let's praise His name!
He is holy, He is almighty.
He is love. He brings hope,
forgiveness, heart cleansing,
peace, and power.
He is our deliverer
and coming King.
Praise His wonderful name!

LUCILLE M. LAW

God's Healing Perspective

The LORD is close to the brokenhearted
and saves those who are crushed in spirit.

PSALM 34:18 NIV

*M*ost of us have had the experience of comforting a small child who has experienced physical or emotional pain. A few minutes in the arms of a loving parent or other caring adult is usually enough to soothe a little person's everyday hurts.

In the same way, God longs to comfort us as we experience emotional pain as adults. He invites us to come to Him for reassurance and encouragement as well as healing. But sometimes the pain runs very deep and is held in place by lies that have been believed and closed up inside. In these cases, God wants to replace those painful lies with healing truth during our time of prayer, whether alone with God or with the help of an experienced minister or counselor.

Don't be afraid to be completely honest with God. He isn't afraid of your strong emotions. As you express to Him what feels true inside, allow Him to enlighten you so that you see things from His healing perspective.

God, some of the lies I want You to replace with Your truth are…

Your love is comfort
in sadness,
quietness in tumult,
rest in weariness,
hope in despair.

MARION C. GARRETTY

Yours to Enjoy

We love because he first loved us.

1 John 4:19 niv

You were created to enjoy a satisfying relationship with God. Almost sounds too good to be true, but it is. More than a life of fun or happiness or making a difference in your world, God created you to enjoy Him.

So how do we enter this satisfying relationship with God? Begin by inviting Him into every area of your life. That might make you a little uncomfortable, but the next step makes the first step easier: Accept the fact that God is crazy about you. You are His heart's delight. That's right. The Creator of the universe deeply enjoys time spent with you. It's very hard to resist someone who cares about you like that.

When something good happens to you, thank Him for making it happen. When you're having a rough day, ask Him for strength. When you need to process your feelings, confide in Him. You don't need to set aside time to tell Him, just tell Him. Over time, you'll discover that He is your deepest satisfaction.

Lord God, I can invite Your presence in my life specifically when…

[God] is looking for people
who will come in simple
dependence upon
His grace, and rest
in simple faith upon
His greatness.
At this very moment,
He's looking at you.

JACK HAYFORD

Beyond Believing

*Now Ezra had determined in his heart
to study the law of the LORD, obey it,
and teach its statutes and ordinances in Israel.*

EZRA 7:10 HCSB

It is one thing to gain understanding. It is quite another thing to live as if you have understanding. And it is something else altogether to help others understand. Gaining insight into God—His ways and His will—may come through various means: study of His Word, listening to sermons, reading books on relevant topics, or even observing God's amazing creation. Your mind gets stretched out of its previous paradigm and expanded to receive the vast revelation of the incredible God that He is.

Taking the next step—putting your understanding into action—requires more than merely an intellectual exercise. Your heart and your will become engaged in the motivation and determination to conform your life to what you have learned. This moves you from the arena of academia into the realm of authentic experience where character is forged, decisions are made, and people are deeply impacted.

But even more—getting beyond yourself—you discover, at last, that helping someone else to know the Lord brings with it a joy and a measure of fulfillment unlike anything you've experienced yet. That joy multiplies—within the community of faith and within the heart of God. Don't settle for mere understanding. Go beyond belief.

Dear Father, I want to go beyond simply believing because…

Our love to God
is measured by our
everyday fellowship
with others
and the love it displays.

ANDREW MURRAY

The Celebration of Obedience

Go your way, eat the fat, drink the sweet, and send portions
to those for whom nothing is prepared; for this day is holy
to our Lord. Do not sorrow, for the joy of the LORD is your strength.

NEHEMIAH 8:10 NKJV

Did you know that God loves to throw parties? If you were brought up to think of Him as austere and unapproachable, you are in for a wonderful surprise. He is, in fact, the author of celebration.

What kinds of things cause God to call for a celebration? When, with willing hearts, God's people joined Him in His mission to rescue, reconcile, and restore His people, His purpose, His cities, and His reign on the earth, His response was overwhelming joy and He regularly threw parties to give it expression. There were parties for celebrating the grain harvest and marriage. Parties for consecrating the tabernacle and the priests. There were parties to celebrate birth and parties to commemorate deliverance from bondage. There was even the weekly celebration of Sabbath—rest.

So how can you get in on the celebration and experience the joy He's planned for you? By committing yourself to God's purposes and spending time with Him, getting to know your role in what He is about here on earth. You'll quickly discover the joy that resides in God's heart when His people get involved in celebrating what He is doing. You'll also discover that the party never ends!

I want to get in on the joy, dear God, by…

God came to us because God
wanted to join us on the road,
to listen to our story,
and to help us realize that
we are not walking in circles
but moving toward the house
of peace and joy.

HENRI J. M. NOUWEN

Beneath the Surface

[Our fathers] disciplined us for a little while
as they thought best; but God disciplines us for our good,
in order that we may share in his holiness.

Hebrews 12:10 niv

When God looks at your life, many things are clearly in focus for Him that may not be on your radar screen at all. Much of life is a process of God bringing those things into focus for you. When difficulties enter your life, God may use these struggles to bring something to your attention that will greatly help you. Like an Olympic athlete in training, God is training you for the life and the eternity that He has planned for you. While the individual ingredients of your life may not be at all pleasant, the final product will be beautiful. God does not enjoy seeing His children in pain. But He may use that pain to bring something into the limelight that He wants to discuss with you.

How do you pray through this? Simply ask. Ask God if there's something—anything—that He wants you to see. As you submit yourself to Him, He will show you the way forward.

God, some things I need to bring into focus are…

For God Himself works
in our souls, in their
deepest depths,
taking increasing control
as we are progressively willing
to be prepared for His wonder.

THOMAS R. KELLY

When we take time
to notice the simple things
in life, we never lack
for encouragement.
We discover we are
surrounded by a limitless
hope that's just wearing
everyday clothes.

To the Heights

We are hard pressed on every side, but not crushed;
perplexed, but not in despair

2 CORINTHIANS 4:8 NIV

The poster in the human resources office showed a three-branched seedling at the base of a giant sequoia. The caption on the poster read "Determination." Webster's Dictionary defines determination as "the act of deciding definitely and firmly."

Living with faith in God is so much more than feeling. It takes determination. Sure, some aspects are easier than others. But to have faith in the face of, say, a cancer diagnosis is one thing; to be joyful in that same circumstance is quite another. Yet as you consistently spend time in prayer—either for yourself or on behalf of someone else who is afflicted—your faith is energized and you understand that God remains in control, no matter how much things seem to be in chaos.

Help your faith grow from a little sapling to the heights of a giant redwood tree by prioritizing your relationship with God. Make your determined, firm decision now to establish faith-filled prayer in your life, in good times or bad.

God, I give You the difficult trials I'm facing today, especially...

[Trials] may come
in abundance.
But they cannot
penetrate into the sanctuary
of the soul when it is settled
in God, and we may
dwell in perfect peace.

HANNAH WHITALL SMITH

Run for the Hills

Be strong and courageous. Do not be afraid or discouraged.
2 CHRONICLES 32:7 NIV

Fear can claw at our minds and hearts and squeeze the joy out of life. If we stop to think about it, most of us fear dozens of things every single day. We fear being late for work, we fear being involved in a car accident, we fear the disapproval of others. Some of us dread dental appointments, financial slowdowns, and aging. Fear is cloaked in big and small packages.

Yet our fear, worry, and apprehension are no surprise to God. He understands us when we balk at challenges or panic when pained. Countless times throughout His Word, God confidently reassures us that we can gain courage and "fear not." Yet He doesn't just command our bravery, He nudges us to let go of our anxiety and apprehensions by shifting our thinking.

How do we practically deal with those never-ending fears? By remembering throughout the day that we are not alone because God—who is infinitely greater than any intimidating person or any daunting situation—is right beside us. When reminded that God is constantly on our side, we can stand up to our fears and watch our worry take a run for the hills.

Lord, I give to You all these things that cause me fear,
worry, and anxiety today…

God Incarnate is the end of fear;
and the heart that realizes that He
is in the midst, that takes heed
to the assurance of His loving presence,
will be quiet in the midst of alarm.

F. B. MEYER

God of All Comfort

I will turn their mourning into joy,
give them consolation, and bring happiness out of grief.
JEREMIAH 31:13 HCSB

At some point in life, death's finality will cover each of our hearts and wrestle with our deepest emotions—we'll lose a grandparent, a parent, a spouse, a child, a friend, a pet. Perhaps you are walking the meandering path of grief right now. Your bruised heart pleads silently for someone to hear your inner agony, "Will this pain ever end?" In your sorrow, you long for the comfort and safety of expressing your tattered emotions without camouflaging how you *really* feel. As much as others care, they cannot fully soothe the depth of your pain.

How reassuring to know that God is that ever-present, safe someone who longs to listen to your pain and alleviate the agony of your loss. He is your trusted traveling companion throughout each step of your journey. Over the coming weeks, months, and years, He will, bit by bit, replace your mourning with joy.

Gladness of heart and a rejoicing spirit may seem impossible right now, but lighter times will eventually lift your heaviness. For the present, simply rest in knowing God empathizes with you because He also lost someone dear to His own heart—His only Son. And through His loss, we receive hope and eternal life.

The sorrows I want You to know about, Lord, are...

Can we find a friend so faithful,
Who will all our sorrows share?
Jesus knows our every weakness,
Take it to the Lord in prayer.

GEORGE SCRIVEN

Having Fun

*Surely you have granted him unending blessings
and made him glad with the joy of your presence.*

PSALM 21:6 NIV

Sometimes God is portrayed as a killjoy. But nothing could be further from the truth. Having fun is one of God's specialties.

Jesus spent a good part of His time going to parties, relaxing, and enjoying life. He knew how to joke around. God rejoices over His children with singing. While God is at home with sorrow and pain, He doesn't camp there. He is, deep inside, happy. He measured everything at the beginning and decided it was worth it all. Heaven is heaven for God as well as man. God deeply enjoys His children, His creation, His own eternal life.

When you pray, you are praying to a God who is happy. He is filled with joy. And He is capable of enjoying life with you. He likes hanging out with you. He's not uptight. He's not hyper spiritual all the time. He knows when to get serious, and He knows when to relax and have fun. If you could see His face right now, more likely than not, He would be smiling.

God, thinking of having fun with You makes me feel…

When we realize
He's bigger than anything
we can get our minds around,
we can begin to relax
and enjoy Him.

PAULA RHINEHART

Praying with Fragility

Trust in him at all times, you people;
pour out your hearts to him, for God is our refuge.

PSALM 62:8 NIV

If humans came with an instruction book, you'd see labels like FRAGILE or HANDLE WITH CARE stamped prominently on the cover. This is shown in the fascinating way the men and women in the Bible prayed. Their vulnerability is there for all to see. They lament and cry out, begging God to know them. Then, before it's all done, they're singing praises about His faithfulness.

The writer of most of the Psalms, David, knew God was listening to Him. In his heartfelt prayers, King David learned of God's dependability, discovered that he could rely on God's kindness, and waited with anticipation for God's answer, even if His response was going to be different than David wanted.

The Lord enjoys this process. Relationship and communication are His inventions, and He loves to live them out with us. Today, share your deepest feelings with God as you seek Him in prayer. No matter how fragile you're feeling, He'll prove the reliability of your trust in Him—and He'll handle you with the utmost care.

God, I will trust You today with my heartfelt prayers for…

The more we depend
on God the more
dependable we find He is.

CLIFF RICHARD

Jumping for Joy

[A] person can pray to God and find favor with him,
they will see God's face and shout for joy.

JOB 33:26 NIV

*D*o you jump for joy? Unless you're naturally over-exuberant (or, perhaps, a sports fan), you probably don't often let your feet leave the ground in a burst of happiness. This is because, generally, your circumstances don't call for such a reaction. Real life, even in cheery moments, is a tad more mundane.

That's what makes the Bible so relevant. It provides basic instruction that you can apply to your everyday existence. When it says to be joyful always with prayer and thanksgiving, God is giving you a way to navigate whatever circumstances come your way. He is suggesting that you, at various times throughout each day, come to Him with a thankful heart because you know He will work all things for your ultimate good. That produces a joyful outlook that's based on how you look at life rather than on what is happening to you at that moment.

So don't just jump for joy. Live in it, and pray confidently for yourself and others—in spite of it all.

Heavenly Father, I want to joyously give thanks to You today for…

It is right and good that we,
for all things, at all times,
and in all places, give thanks
and praise to You, O God.
We worship You, we confess to You,
we praise you... Maker,
Nourisher, Guardian, Healer,
Lord, and Father of all.

LANCELOT ANDREWES

The soft, sweet summer
was warm and glowing,
Bright were the blossoms
on every bough:
I trusted Him when the roses
were blooming;
I trust Him now.

L. B. COWMAN

Praying Through Grief

My comfort in my suffering is this:
Your promise preserves my life.

PSALM 119:50 NIV

*G*rief and loss enter everyone's life sooner or later. As a person of prayer, you have your relationship with God to fall back on during these difficult times.

God is the God of all comfort, and He understands sorrow. His heart aches when you are hurting. He will be with you when others can't. He alone stands on both sides of life and death. He alone has the power to wipe away every tear and offer you hope and a future even in time of loss.

Anger is one of the natural stages of grief. It's very common to be angry with God, and it is okay and even healthy to share that anger with Him. God is not afraid of your anger. He is not put off by it. As you pour out your heart to Him and find the edges of that anger, He can help you find the comforting truth that goes deeper than your loss, and He will ultimately point the way back to joy.

God, when I experience grief, help me…

There are those who
suffer greatly, and yet,
through the recognition
that pain can be a thread
in the pattern of God's
weaving, find the way
to a fundamental joy.

Lower Your Stress Points

I will greatly rejoice in the LORD,
my soul shall be joyful in my God.

ISAIAH 61:10 NKJV

Imagine taking a stress test ascribing points to each of your situations and discovering your score was in the danger zone. Ever feel that way as life presses in?

If today's psychiatrists had designated stress points to the problems the apostle Paul faced in the Bible (shipwrecks, imprisonment, starvation, physical exhaustion, etc.) his score would've been so far off the scale they would have expected him to disintegrate. But Paul said that, despite his troubles, he had boundless joy!

Happiness (based on circumstances) goes up and down like a thermometer. True joy comes through faith in God, knowing that He loves you, answers your prayers, and works things for your good. If your life is filled with bad news, turn your mind to God's good news and thank Him for His benefit in your life. You'll probably find there are more benefits than you think. Then, once you have prayed for yourself, ask God to work in the lives of your loved ones, that they'll find true joy in His eternal truths.

God, I give thanks to You today for the wonderful benefits of…

Joy is more than my
spontaneous expression
of laughter, gaiety,
and lightness. It is deeper
than an emotional
expression of happiness.
Joy is a growing,
evolving manifestation of God
in my life as I walk with Him.

BONNIE MONSON

Sadness that Turns to Joy

Those who sow with tears will reap with songs of joy.
PSALM 126:5 NIV

A godly prayer life has many dynamics. Praising. Asking. Listening. Confessing. But when was the last time you truly grieved for your own missteps and waywardness or that of someone else?

In the Bible, the prophet Daniel grieved for his nation's stubborn nature. Even though they had been held captive by a neighboring superpower for seventy years, they would not turn to God. So Daniel pleaded with the Lord in prayer. He so identified with his nation's faults he confessed them as though he had committed them himself.

If your family or friends who are living in a way they shouldn't or are experiencing the consequences of their own stubborn ways, grieve for them in prayer. Take their needs before God in caring passion. If there's something you know is not right in your own life, pray for yourself with the same attitude. As surely as your tears bring sorrow, you can be confident that your mourning will turn to joy as God speaks and brings His restoration.

Dear Father, three people and circumstances
that I can grieve in prayer for are…

We are God's fellow workers,
and as such we turn
to prayer to equip us
for the partnership.

PHILIP YANCEY

Stop, Drop, and Pray

Cast all your anxiety on him because he cares for you.
1 PETER 5:7 NIV

You can always churn with anxiety about something—illness, loss, a financial setback, terrorism. Anxiety is a common stressor for many of us, even if it's just a tiny nagging whisper. At times you may find yourself waking up in the middle of the night with a daytime concern now magnified. What can be done with budding panic at three in the morning?

Anxiety creeps in where control issues have left the door ajar. It hooks in to that part of you that wants circumstances to go your way and keeps you obsessing about the outcome. When you're ready to let go of handling distress on your own, pour out your heart to God. He totally understands what you need. He knows and is compassionate about what's bothering you. You can count on Him to act.

Just a simple request will do, nothing formal or fancy. There's no ritual or perfect prayer wording required. You can tell God in elaborate detail or just get to the point. When you're done, thank Him for all His wonderful blessings and for who He is. Then let Him handle things while you move calmly forward with your day.

Dear God, here are my anxious thoughts…

Oh, let the place
of secret prayer
become to me
the most beloved
spot on earth.

ANDREW MURRAY

All Around You
Consider the lilies of the field, how they grow.

MATTHEW 6:28 NKJV

*H*ave you ever watched hawks soar, riding the thermals in great easy circles in the sky? Have you seen the leaves of the cottonwood tree dance in a summer breeze? There's something about nature that brings the presence of God near. His signature is everywhere—in the moonlight sparkling on the water, in the wildflowers jostling each other in the wind, the trails leading off into the woods. As you walk with God, marveling at His creation all around you, you get a sense of His giddy joy in His work.

It's renewing to drink in the beauty of all living things. This is probably why so many people choose beaches and mountains and parks as vacation destinations.

Give yourself an opportunity to enjoy the outdoors where and when you can. As you do, invite God into the experience. Make it a different kind of prayer—one where requests are not so much on the agenda, but rather quiet enjoyment of each other and of God's artistry. You will walk away enriched and restored.

God, open my eyes to better appreciate…

Beauty puts a face on God.
When we gaze at nature,
at a loved one, at a work of art,
our soul immediately recognizes
and is drawn to the face of God.

MARGARET BROWNLEY

Rising Above It All

He will yet fill your mouth with laughter
and your lips with shouts of joy.

JOB 8:21 NIV

*H*appiness is like a slippery eel. Just when you think you have hold of it, it slides from your grasp and slithers away. When the situation changes, there goes your happiness!

Joy is different. The world can be crashing down around you, yet you can be joyful when you place your trust in God. It's possible that you have allowed circumstances to rob you of the joy God wants you to have. It's easy to lose joy if you look only at what's happening around you. The Bible says we are to be joyful always. Rather than living under our circumstances, God wants us to live above them by keeping our eyes on Him.

Right now, thank the Lord for allowing the current conditions and events in your life, realizing He has something for you to learn or accomplish through them. Then pray with that same attitude for the circumstances your friends and family are facing, knowing God is still accomplishing His purposes for them as well. Have a joyful heart in Him, and don't let it slip away.

God, please help me in circumstances
that are troubling me today such as…

God has a wonderful plan
for each person.... He knew
even before He created
this world what beauty
He would bring forth from our lives.

Louise B. Wyly

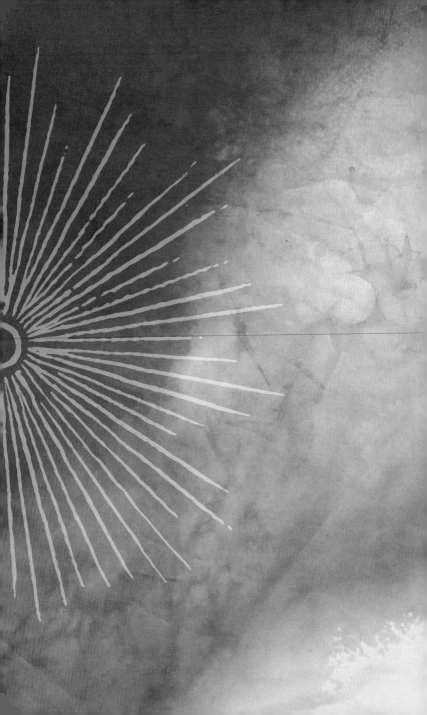

Satisfy us in the morning
with your unfailing love,
that we may sing for joy
and be glad all our days.

PSALM 90:14 NIV

Less Is More

The LORD said to Gideon, "You have too many people
for Me to hand the Midianites over to you,
or else Israel might brag: 'I did it myself.'"
JUDGES 7:2 HCSB

Some days you have fewer resources than you think you need to win the day. You get up in the morning wishing you had a few more minutes of sleep, a bit more energy, and more gas in the tank. The decisions you must make would be easier with more information. You're feeling a bit off your game. That can be a good thing. When you have less, you're stretched to find resources. God longs for you to rely on His resources for victory. His supply is limitless, but it's easy to forget that when you have all you need.

When people struggle through something together, it brings them closer. A group of soldiers is forever bonded after facing intense challenges together, relying on each other's strengths to win the battle. God wants you to win. And He wants you to have the joy of seeing Him personally come through for you.

In a quiet moment today, take stock of your resources. If you see you're coming up short on what it takes to overcome, believe that God wants victory for you and He wants to prove afresh His might in your life.

Today, Lord, I need Your resources of…

Do not strive in your own strength;
cast yourself at the feet of
the Lord Jesus, and wait upon
Him in the sure confidence that
He is with you, and works in you.
Strive in prayer; let faith
fill your heart so will you
be strong in the Lord,
and in the power of His might.

ANDREW MURRAY

Strong Arms

He tends his flock like a shepherd:
He gathers the lambs in his arms and carries them
close to his heart; he gently leads those that have young.

Isaiah 40:11 niv

If you've ever comforted a crying baby or young child, you know how little ones love to snuggle in close to you. The longer the infant or toddler remains in your arms, the more the sobs lessen and the child's previously tense and squirming body relaxes. There's just something soothing about being held by someone you trust.

The same can be said of your relationship with God. He knows just when to let your tears fall and when to let you have your own tantrum. He also knows just when to draw near and enfold you in a comforting embrace. When you feel like you're limping and crawling, He knows just when to pick you up and carry you until you've regained your footing.

Do you need God to point you in the right direction or come alongside you with a calming hug? He longs to reassure you and sustain you no matter what unfolds in your life. There's no need to wait until you're surprised by tough news or overjoyed with unexpected blessings before you lean upon God. The more you get to know God each new day, the more you will entrust yourself to His all-powerful arms and His loving heart.

Lord, these are the situations I need You to carry me through…

There is an activity of the spirit,
silent, unseen, which must be
the dynamic of any form of truly
creative, fruitful trust. When we commit
a predicament, a possibility, a person
to God in genuine confidence, we do not
merely step aside and tap our foot until
God comes through. We remain involved.
We remain in contact with God
in gratitude and praise. But we do this
without anxiety, without worry.

EUGENIA PRICE

Sing a New Song

He has put a new song in my mouth—praise to our God;
many will see it and fear, and will trust in the LORD.

PSALM 40:3 NKJV

Have you ever made up a song to God? One of the invitations the Bible extends is this: Sing to the Lord a new song. Parents understand what a treasure this can be. A happy and contented child will sometimes break into song—a new song, spontaneous, from the heart.

Even if you have no musical talent, you can still sing to God when you're alone with Him. Song captures human emotion and experience in a way that words alone cannot. Your song could express whatever is going on inside you—quiet contentment, a deep longing, righteous indignation, or joyful celebration. No one will judge your vocal performance, so you can be free to unselfconsciously sing out whatever is deep inside.

Your song might be the gateway to a whole new dimension of experiencing God. Go ahead! Let the lyrics come and offer them up to God.

God, when I think about singing to You,
the words I want to sing are…

Let us give all that lies
within us...to pure praise,
to pure loving adoration,
and to worship from
a grateful heart a heart
that is trained to look up.

AMY CARMICHAEL

Love covers all

Above all, love each other deeply,
because love covers over a multitude of sins.

1 PETER 4:8 NIV

You know how miscommunication and mistakes can fuel the flames of a smoldering misunderstanding.

Words somehow turn heated. Feelings quickly singe. Maybe that's why God emphasizes love so much in the Bible. He knows us all too well. Like the gentle father that He is, He reminds us that first and foremost we are to love one another. It is love that will keep us faithful, keep us joyful, keep us tuned in to heavenly things.

You may never have considered all the things love can do. When someone speaks unfavorably about you, love can kindle forgiveness. When a person deeply wounds you, love can bring healing. When you blow it and offend someone, love can help you find your way to remorse and forgiveness. Love can make friends of enemies and break the bonds of prejudice.

But you can't generate restorative love on your own. It takes God's long-suffering, gentle love to cool the heat of anger and heal broken hearts. His love reaches further than you could ever imagine. It has been called the mightiest force in all the universe. Give it first place in all your relationships.

I believe that love is the most important thing in the world because…

Lord...give me the gift of faith
to be renewed and shared
with others each day. Teach me
to live this moment only,
looking neither to the past
with regret, nor the future
with apprehension. Let love
be my aim and my life a prayer.

Roseann Alexander-Isham

When We Stumble

*I have no greater joy than to hear
that my children are walking in the truth.*

3 JOHN 1:4 NIV

How does a child learn to walk? By falling down! In the same way, as we learn to walk with God, we will stumble. We will make mistakes. We will make bad choices that have undesirable consequences for ourselves and others.

What does a good coach do when players make mistakes? Does he rub their nose in it? Does he kick them off the team? Does he write the word "failure" over their lives? No! He meets the problems head on, turns them into lessons, and moves on.

This is one way to recognize the Spirit of God in our lives. When we blow it (and we will), there's always forward momentum in how God deals with it. He doesn't leave us in condemnation. He brings us to the place where we can face our wrongdoing squarely, do what's possible to make it right, learn from our error, and move on. If a voice inside your head is loading you with condemnation without giving you a way out, that is not the Spirit of God. God restores us.

Have you done wrong? Rush back into God's presence. God will receive you. He will repair you. You will be whole once again.

Lord, when I stumble, my first response is to…

God doesn't remember my mistakes.
For all the things He does do,
this is one thing He refuse to do.
He refuses to keep a list of my wrongs.
When I ask for forgiveness He doesn't
pull out a clipboard and say,
"But I've already forgiven him
for that five hundred and sixteen times."
He doesn't remember.

MAX LUCADO

A Song in Your Heart

The LORD is my strength and my shield;
my heart trusts in Him, and I am helped.
Therefore my heart rejoices, and I praise Him with my song.

PSALM 28:7 HCSB

Do you nurture an attitude of gratitude? Sometimes the daily grind can erode your joy, making you forget the blessings and benefits of a life redeemed by Jesus. Whiny teenagers, insensitive spouses, harried commutes, unremitting financial pressures, and over-scheduled lives create noise—external and internal—that muffles God's voice. *Thank God for what?* you might wonder to yourself. *All my stress?*

Often we trudge through life with a dejected gait. If we're not careful we can start to sound like gloomy Eeyore, Winnie the Pooh's pal, who resigns much of life to his trademark, "Ohhh-kayyy." You, on the other hand, were created to keep a song in your heart, even if on some days it's hard to sing.

Each day is an invitation to re-order your life to make room for gratitude to God. As you settle down for prayer, worship, or Bible study, begin by spending time thanking God for the little things. Your ability to read, your home, the people who love you. Contemplate all the simple things that bring you unexpected joys. In no time, you'll find yourself refreshed with a grateful heart and moving from a drab "Ohhh-kayyy" to a delighted "Ohhh-yeaaa!"

Please restore my joy, God. I praise You for…

...I will accept Your will,
whatever that may be. Thank You
for counting this act of my will
as the decision of the real person even
when my emotions protest.
It is You, Lord, God, who alone
are worthy of worship. I bend
the knee with thanksgiving that
this too will "work together for good."

CATHERINE MARSHALL

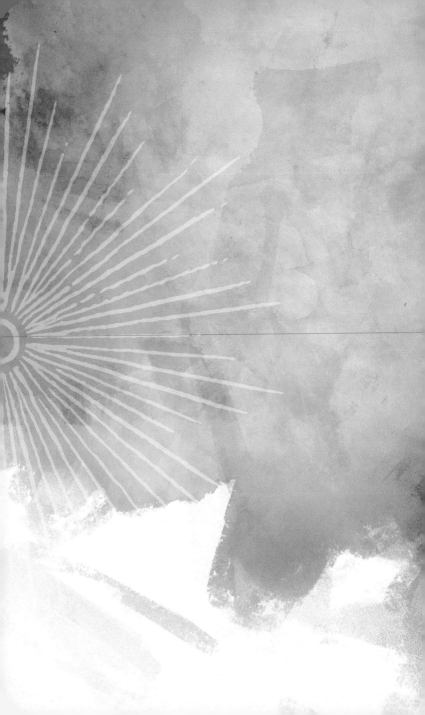

Some days, it is enough encouragement just to watch the clouds break up and disappear, leaving behind a blue patch of sky and bright sunshine that is so warm upon my face. It's a glimpse of divinity; a kiss from heaven.

More Wonderful Reality

We have different gifts, according to the grace given to each of us.

ROMANS 12:6 NIV

*E*veryone is gifted with different talents. You may have a gift for speaking in public. Someone else may have a gift for writing letters of encouragement. God has also given every person a specific opportunity for service to others. And even if you think your gift is small or trivial, it could be the very thing that God employs to draw someone to His love.

Yet the delight of using that gift pales in comparison to the greater gift of eternal life. In the Bible, we read that Jesus sent out seventy-two of His followers to serve in the towns and villages He was about to visit. They were thrilled by the success they were having, but Jesus quickly put things in perspective, saying that their joy should not rest in the supernatural, but in the more wonderful reality of their salvation.

Today, appreciate your talents and abilities, but don't find your happiness in them. Thank God that you have been forgiven. Then pray that He would use you—and your talents and abilities—to help others discover His forgiving love.

Allow me today, God, to show Your love to…

God gave me my gifts.
I will do all I can
to show Him how grateful
I am to Him.

GRACE LIVINGSTON HILL

Steady On

LORD, how long will You forget me, forever?
How long will You hide Your face from me?
PSALM 13:1 HCSB

Feeling forgotten and invisible to God and to people you care about hurts. Pain isolates and cocoons you from the world, whether its source is emotional or physical. When trouble comes your way, it may seem like a gray curtain is drawn around you. You can see out, but you don't feel anyone can see in.

Believe it or not, even Jesus had that feeling. As He was on the cross, He cried out asking why the Father had turned away. You can be assured that the Son of God understands how your abandonment feels since He experienced this emotion Himself. There will be dark times of the soul when you'll feel alone, as if even God Himself has left you. In the midst of that darkness, stay steady. Keep on doing what you know to be right. Keep on spending time with God every day, meditating on a verse or two to strengthen your faith. Hang on to your trust in God. The light is coming back as sure as the sun rises after the darkness of night. In time, you will stand victorious in the Spirit, knowing that even if your feelings indicated otherwise, God never deserted you.

This is what I will do today, Lord, to stay steady...

I believe in the sun even
if it isn't shining.
I believe in love
even when I am alone.
I believe in God
even when He is silent.

Evidence of a Generous God

If any of you lacks wisdom, you should ask God, who gives generously to all without finding fault, and it will be given to you.
JAMES 1:5 NIV

When you think of God's generosity, what's the first thing that comes to your mind? Many consider it to be His material blessings—the nicer house than you ever thought you'd be living in, a car that runs smoothly, or maybe a totally unexpected raise. But God's generosity extends beyond the material world. The evidence of His generosity lies in the essence of who you are.

Through your relationship with God, you acquire unseen traits, character qualities, and values that become evident to others through your actions. Every wise decision you make in difficult circumstances reveals how generous God has been with His wisdom. Every time you forgive someone who in reality deserves your scorn and revenge, it shows how generous God has been in giving you the ability to extend forgiveness and mercy—undeserved kindness.

But those attributes don't come to you as if by magic. They become integrated into your character and your spirit as you spend intentional, purposeful time with God. You can get to know *about* God's attributes through personal study and the teaching of others, but to make them your own, you need to spend time alone with Him, allowing Him to lavish on you the qualities than come from Him alone.

Lord, among the evidences of Your generosity in my life are…

Strength, rest,
guidance, grace,
help, sympathy, love—
all from God to us!
What a list of blessings!

EVELYN STENBOCK

Thank God—for Everything

Giving thanks always for everything
to God the Father in the name of our Lord Jesus Christ.
EPHESIANS 5:20 HCSB

It's been said that gratitude is our most direct line to God. Pouring out your gratitude to God will often bring you immediately into His presence; in fact, whenever you feel that there's some distance between you and God, begin thanking Him—genuinely, from your heart—and see how quickly that gap disappears.

But what about those times when your life isn't running so smoothly? How can you honestly express your gratitude to God when you can't find much to be thankful for? You could start by thanking Him for being there during the rough patches, for welcoming you into His presence so you can unload your burdens on Him, for the good that will ultimately come from life's difficulties. Once you start thanking Him in that way, you're likely to find even more reasons to be grateful.

When you cultivate a grateful attitude during the good times, thanking God during the not-so-good times will come much more easily. Many people have found it helpful to keep a gratitude journal, a place where they keep a running account of everything they have to be thankful for. During hard times, your list of blessings can become your prayer of thanksgiving.

Today I am thankful to You, Lord, for…

And when I give thanks
for the seemingly microscopic,
I make a place for God
to grow within me.

ANN VOSKAMP

Celebrate Anyway

Though the fig tree does not bud and there is no fruit on the vines, though the olive crop fails and the fields produce no food, though there are no sheep in the pen and no cattle in the stalls, yet I will triumph in Yahweh; I will rejoice in the God of my salvation!

HABAKKUK 3:17–18 HCSB

Fair-weather friends are a pain. Ever have one? You know, the kind that stick with you when everything is even-keeled, but when trouble comes into your life they seem to fade into the next dimension.

God's not keen on us being fickle either. After all He did to rescue us, God wants friends that are in it for the long haul. He wants friends who believe in Him at all times.

No matter how much we wish it weren't so, troubling times can stir up feelings of being abandoned by God. And the devil will milk that feeling by hissing into our thoughts: *God doesn't actually love me, because if He did, wouldn't I have more money / a better boss / a better marriage / a spouse?*

When everything seems to turn sour, don't ditch your faith. Hang on to that part of you that knows God is good, that knows His love is the best thing that's ever happened to you. Build your faith and your friendship with God by celebrating His extraordinary presence in your dark times. When you sense life is drying up around you, God will always be your steady source of joy.

In the midst of trouble, I choose to celebrate because…

Even when all we see
are the tangled threads
on the backside
of life's tapestry,
we know that God is good
and is out to do us good always.

RICHARD J. FOSTER

Joy in God

Look on us with favor, LORD.
You have put more joy in my heart
than they have when their grain and new wine abound.

PSALM 4:6–7 HCSB

Rising up at morning's first light, anticipation fills my heart as I prepare to sit with God during the earliest moments of the day, basking in His sunlight. I turn on a lamp, wash the sleep from my eyes, and pour my first cup of coffee, running through the day's agenda in my mind briefly as I settle into my chair.

I am aware that the disposition of my heart is bent toward one direction or another as a result of yesterday's events and today's pressures. Somewhere in the tension between the two, I open myself up to God and let His light shine in on me, washing over my inner being with rejuvenation and joy.

I sense His countenance in the gentleness of the rising sun—His joy in creation coming alive with the dawn's new light. I join Him rejoicing over the simple pleasures of nature: the dew sparkling on the grass, the cheerful song of the birds perched on a limb nearby, the gentle breeze wafting through the window by my chair.

Prayers of thanksgiving and praise well up in my heart and find expression in spontaneous worship without effort. I have awakened to find that God is already awake to me.

Thank You, God, that You never sleep and You're watching over…

Lift up your eyes.
Your heavenly Father
waits to bless you—
in inconceivable ways
to make your life what
you never dreamed it could be.

ANNE ORTLUND

Every good gift
and every perfect gift
is from above,
and comes down from
the Father of lights,
with whom there is no variation
or shadow of turning.

James 1:17 nkjv